SUCCESSFUL GRANT APPLICATIONS

BULLET GUIDE

Hodder Education, 338 Euston Road, London NW1 3BH

Hodder Education is an Hachette UK company

First published in UK 2012 by Hodder Education

This edition published 2012

Also available in ebook

British Library Cataloguing in Publication Data: a catalogue record for this title is available from the British Library.

10 9 8 7 6 5 4 3 2 1

The publisher has used its best endeavours to ensure that any website addresses referred to in this book are correct and active at the time of going to press. However, the publisher and the author have no responsibility for the websites and can make no guarantee that a site will remain live or that the content will remain relevant, decent or appropriate.

The publisher has made every effort to mark as such all words which it believes to be trademarks. The publisher should also like to make it clear that the presence of a word in the book, whether marked or unmarked, in no way affects its legal status as a trademark.

Every reasonable effort has been made by the publisher to trace the copyright holders of material in this book. Any errors or omissions should be notified in writing to the publisher, who will endeavour to rectify the situation for any reprints and future editions.

Hachette UK's policy is to use papers that are natural, renewable and recyclable products and made from wood grown in sustainable forests. The logging and manufacturing processes are expected to conform to the environmental regulations of the country of origin.

www.hoddereducation.co.uk

Typeset by Stephen Rowling/Springworks

Printed in Spain

SUCCESSFUL GRANT APPLICATIONS

BULLET GUIDE

Ann Gawthorpe

Acknowledgements

I would like to thank the following people for all their help and advice:

Sarah Boyce, fundraiser; Sheila Davidson, fundraiser; Sally Dubery, Chief Officer, Voluntary Action Mid Surrey; Ray Emmans, Fund Manager, Windsor and Maidenhead Voluntary Action; Ian Ferguson, Grants Advisor, Preston Council for Voluntary Services; Martha Langley, volunteer with various mental health charities; Tony Moulin, chairman of YACWAG (Yatton and Congresbury Wildlife Action Group); Arsen Poghosyan, Funding and Information Officer, Brentwood Council for Voluntary Services; and Matthew Robinson, fundraiser for a telephone advice service.

And thanks to Lesley Bown for her help and support.

About the author

As chairman and then treasurer of the committee that built a village hall in her village, Ann Gawthorpe was involved not only in helping to get National Lottery funding but also in finding matching funding. She understands how essential it is to get the application process right, how to deal with rejection and how to present different aspects of the project so that it appeals to a variety of funders.

Contents

Introduction

Despite credit crunches, cutbacks and cash shortages it is still possible to obtain **grants** to fund your **projects**. According to various websites there are over 8,000 grant-making bodies. It might take a bit more time, effort and stamina but there is money out there to be had.

To minimize the risk of failure it is absolutely essential to do your **homework** so that you apply to the right funder for your project. Some funders will give money only for a specific item and not for the running costs of the project. Others are region specific or will give only to a registered charity, not a group or individuals. Some want to see that you have matching funding in place, others don't. However, all want to see the **most benefit** for their money and are looking to fund projects that will have a **lasting impact** – and will benefit as many people as possible.

Setting up a project is like starting up a business, and it requires you to be as **professional** as possible. You and your committee may be asking for thousands of pounds, and funders want to know that their money is in **safe hands** and will be wisely spent. Rather than going for one large grant from one funder you might be more successful going for smaller grants from several sources.

The good news is that most funding bodies have **websites**. Many have helpful **advice** and **guidelines** to help you fill in the application forms and many allow you to apply online. Just one word of warning – smaller funders and databases do sometimes disappear, and some of those in this book may have done so by the time you have read it.

But don't be deterred – if you have a **distinctive project**, lots of **enthusiasm** and plenty of **determination**, you will be successful.

1 First steps

What grant makers are looking for

Whatever your project, there are some essential steps to take if you are to be successful in attracting grants

Although there are still funders with money to support **worthwhile** projects, the pot is getting smaller and the demands on it are getting bigger. Those who succeed in getting grants are those who have done their **homework**. They are also those who understand that running a project is like **running a business** and has to be done as **professionally** as possible.

In this chapter we will look at:

* how to **analyse** your project
* the importance of **forward planning**
* the importance of having a **viable** business plan
* the importance of committee members' **skills and talents**
* the importance of **research**
* creating a **realistic** budget
* allowing **time** to find funders
* drawing on other groups' **experience**.

Funders want to be certain that their money is going to do the **most good**, to the **greatest number** of deserving people, and will have a **long-lasting impact**. If you can satisfy these **requirements**, you should be successful in getting grants.

Analyse your project

Firstly, put yourself in the funders' shoes and be **realistic** – why should they give you their money? They have a limited amount to give away and hundreds of groups asking for it. They will want to know:

* What makes your project **essential**?
* How many **people** will it help?
* Do they want or need your **help**?
* What is **distinctive** about your plans?
* Have you checked that there is nothing **similar** in your area?
* What will happen if your project doesn't get off the ground?

> **TOP TIP**
> Check on the Charity Commission website
> (www.charity-commission.gov.uk) to see if
> there are already similar charities.

Like running a race, you will need the ability, expertise and **stamina** to complete the project.

Take time to **plan** your funding campaign. It is better to spend a few hours, days or even weeks getting it right rather than sending off masses of applications for grants that will have little chance of success.

Take advantage of all the help which is available out there.

Be professional
Running a project is like running a small business and must be treated just as seriously

It is essential to put your project on a **professional** footing.

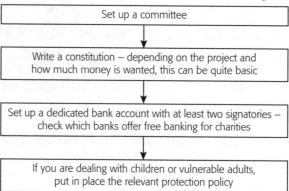

Set up a committee

↓

Write a constitution – depending on the project and how much money is wanted, this can be quite basic

↓

Set up a dedicated bank account with at least two signatories – check which banks offer free banking for charities

↓

If you are dealing with children or vulnerable adults, put in place the relevant protection policy

6

If you want to set up a charity, or if your group will be raising £5,000 a year or more, refer to Chapter 2.

Evaluate your committee members' **strengths**. If the committee has no record of raising money, funders may want to know what **expertise** and skills committee members have in handling large sums of money and seeing the project through – for example, running a small business or being in the building trade.

> **To win the jackpot, funders like to see a track record. If the committee doesn't have one, because it is new, funders will look at the skills of the committee members. It is worth bearing this in mind when forming a committee.**
>
> Tony Moulin, chairman of YACWAG, a local wildlife action group

Have a plan

It may seem obvious, but it is essential to write a project plan (think of it as a business plan).

Writing it down will clarify exactly what you want to achieve.

Firstly, how do you know what is needed? Have you:

1 carried out any **research**?
2 done a **survey**?

Secondly, having proved the need, describe exactly what the project is about and who will **benefit** from it.

Thirdly, draw up a budget. Do you need money for:

* a one-off grant for a building or equipment?
* ongoing financial help?
* overheads and running costs?

Your budget must be **accurate** and realistic with evidence to back it up. There is no point in underbudgeting to help your application: if you do, your project might run out of money before it can be completed.

Don't forget to **plan** for future costs.

TOP TIP
Ask your local Voluntary Action Group for help. It can be found in the telephone directory or via the National Association for Volunteers and Community Action website: www.navca.org.uk (see Chapter 7).

Research grant makers

Allow plenty of **time**. There are more than 8,000 grant-making bodies – luckily there are directories and databases (see Chapter 7) that can help point you towards the most appropriate ones for your project. But, even when you have found a funder willing to give you a grant, it could take months before the money arrives in your bank. Some may respond in a few days, others may make decisions only three or four times a year.

Read the application form carefully so that you know how long you will have to wait for an answer. You may have to look for another funder if it is too long.

10

Finding funders is time consuming, and there are no short cuts:

- ☑ **Network** with other groups to see where they got their funding from.
- ☑ **Learn** from their experiences.
- ☑ Make a list of potential funders.
- ☑ Include local and regional funders as well as national grant makers.
- ☑ Check that they are **still giving** grants.
- ☑ Check that you comply with their criteria.
- ☑ Check to see what other projects they have recently funded.
- ☑ **Keep a record** of those you reject – you don't want to look at them twice.

> **TOP TIP**
> Spread the **workload** round the committee –
> don't leave it all to one person.

2 Setting up a charity

Pros and cons of charitable status

Deciding whether or not to become a charity is a key decision for any fundraising group

Everyone has an idea of what a **charity** is, but in law the term has a specific meaning. In England and Wales any group, provided that its remit complies with the **Charities Act** 2006, can call itself a charity. In Scotland and Northern Ireland, it has to register with the relevant authority before it can do so.

Groups that fall outside the above definition are called **fundraising groups**.

In this chapter we will also look at the advantages and disadvantages of being a registered charity.

Advantages	Disadvantages
Exemption from tax	Registration is complex
Can claim Gift Aid	Requires trustees
Fundraising is easier	Needs a formal constitution

Some groups don't have to register as they are 'excepted', such as the Church of England, or can't register because they are 'exempt', such as universities.

What is a charity?

A charity, as currently defined by the Charities Act 2006, is an institution that is established for charitable purposes and **benefits the public**. The Act lists 13 charitable purposes, ranging from the advancement of education to the arts, and from amateur sports to animal welfare.

In England and Wales a group can call itself a charity provided its aims and objectives comply with the Act. In England and Wales it isn't possible to register a charity until it has an income of £5,000 – and when that figure is reached it has to apply for **registration by law**.

In Scotland and Northern Ireland, groups have to register with the Office of the Scottish Charity Regulator (www.oscr.org.uk) or the Charity Commission for Northern Ireland (www.charitycommissionni.org.uk), respectively, to be called a charity – even if they have raised no money – otherwise they are called fundraising groups.

Registration isn't automatic – if any of your organization's activities or purposes are considered not to be charitable and of benefit to the public, the Charity Commission (www.charity-commission.gov.uk) could turn down your application.

Excepted charities are still regulated by the Charity Commission and may have to provide information about their activities. Exempt charities are not regulated by the Charity Commission but are supervised by other regulators.

Registering a charity

Registration can be done online on the Charity Commission website

Go to the Charity Commission website (www.charity-commission.gov.uk), click on 'Starting up a Charity', and choose 'Do I need to register?' from the menu.

Not all groups can register, even if they want to. You can't register if:

- ☒ you are fundraising for another charity
- ☒ your group is part of a larger organization that is already registered – unless you have your own bank account
- ☒ your group is an **'excepted'** charity such as Guides or Scouts or some churches and chapels, including the Church of England
- ☒ your group is 'exempt', such as governing bodies of voluntary or foundation schools.

However, unregistered charities can also apply for **tax relief** from HM Revenue and Customs and can use their tax number as evidence to funders of their charitable status.

The advantages are:

* Some grant makers will give money only to registered charities.
* Registration gives **status and credibility** to your project.
* People are more likely to offer time, energy or money.
* Charities are exempt from income, corporation and capital gains tax.
* Charities can increase their income through Gift Aid.

The disadvantages are:

* legal obligations
* no political activities
* increased paperwork
* requirement to provide annual accounts if the income is more than £10,000
* trustees have more **responsibilities** in law
* Charity Commissioners have powers to intervene if things go wrong.

Appointing trustees

Trustees are the **governing body** of the charity. It is their responsibility to see that the charity is run properly. They are also responsible for managing staff and volunteers and making decisions about what the charity does.

All committee members have a **duty of care** to their organization, but trustees have legal duties and responsibilities. They must ensure that their charity:

1 **complies with the law** relating to fundraising
2 prepares an annual report on its achievements and an annual return
3 remains true to its aims and objectives
4 remains **solvent**
5 avoids activities that might put its funds, assets or **reputation at risk**.

20

Trustees have a **personal liability** if they make the wrong decisions and, for example, run the charity into debt; however, it is possible to take out insurance against this.

If your charity is working with young people or vulnerable adults, the trustees will need to be checked by the **Criminal Records Bureau** before the charity can be registered.

Choose trustees who will bring **skills and experience** to the board. They can be found by personal recommendation, word of mouth or advertising.

TOP TIP
Remember that not all committee members may want to become trustees if their charity has to become registered.

Writing a constitution

A charity with income under £5,000 a year will need only a simple **constitution** or **governing document**.

It should include:

- ☑ **a name** – check that no other charity is using it
- ☑ the **aims and objectives** of the charity
- ☑ what powers the trustees have
- ☑ who can be a member
- ☑ the date of the **annual general meeting**
- ☑ the make-up of the committee and method for choosing members
- ☑ the number of meetings
- ☑ the banking requirements and **who can sign cheques**
- ☑ the auditing of accounts
- ☑ when and how changes to the constitution can be made
- ☑ a dissolution clause
- ☑ what will happen to any unused money.

1 Include all your members when putting the document together so that everyone is clear on what the charity's **aims and objectives** are.
2 Formally **adopt it** at a public meeting and have all committee members sign and date it.

There are samples on the Charity Commission website, or you could ask your local voluntary action group for an example, or key 'Constitutions' into a search engine.

If you think in the future your charity is going to have more than £5,000 a year and will need to be registered with the Charity Commission, then it is better to use a constitution advised by it rather than having to make changes on registration.

Martha Langley, volunteer with various mental health charities

3 Lottery funding

Looking for National Lottery funding

There are many different National Lottery programmes to choose from

The first port of call for getting grants used to be local councils, but recent cutbacks mean that people now look at **National Lottery funding** as a starting point.

But, although the money comes from one central source, that is the money raised each week from the sale of National Lottery tickets, the distribution is via **independent bodies**.

Lottery funding (www.lotteryfunding.org.uk) is a joint website run by all the National Lottery funders.

At the time of writing there are 13 National Lottery funders who distribute the money to good causes. In this chapter we will be looking at:

* Awards for All
* The Big Lottery Fund
* Heritage Lottery Fund
* Sports England.

Each of these funders has **specific criteria** that have to be met. These can vary among England, Scotland, Ireland and Wales.

Some offers are also time limited, so what was available last month might not be available next month. Others are set up for specific purposes and, when that is reached, they are closed to new applicants.

But, as one door closes another one opens, and **new funds** become available.

Awards for All

Awards for All (www.awardsforall.org.uk) covers the whole of the UK, although each country has a slightly different scheme.

It funds small **community-based** projects that will improve communities and the lives of the people who live in them.

In England these projects should specifically:

1 give people better chances in life
2 form stronger communities
3 improve rural and urban environments
4 create healthier and more active people and communities.

* You can apply only if you are a **community group**, a not-for-profit group, a parish or town council, a health body or a school, depending on which country you live in.
* You don't have to be a registered charity.
* The amount of money granted ranges from £300 up to a maximum of £10,000 in 1 year.
* Further grants can be applied for in following years.
* You can apply at any time online, and the **application forms** can be downloaded from the website.
* You should hear whether you are successful or not within 6 weeks.
* You don't require **matching funding**.

Raise your organisation's profile in the local community – it will help your application if you're known.

Martha Langley, volunteer with various mental health charities

Heritage Lottery Fund

This is the largest dedicated funder of the UK's heritage. Its remit is wide and ranges from historic buildings to cultural traditions, and oral history to landscapes, parks and gardens.

Projects must fit into one of eight programmes. The one of most interest to smaller groups is 'Your Heritage', which is for voluntary and community groups and first-time applicants. It offers grants ranging from £3,000 to £50,000 for projects relating to the local, regional and national heritage of the UK and which help people to learn about, look after and celebrate heritage in a fun and enjoyable way.

There are no deadlines for applications, and decisions are made within 10 weeks.

Its main programme, 'Heritage Grants', gives grants of over £50,000 for projects that:

* help people learn about their own and other people's heritage
* conserve the UK's heritage for present and future generations to enjoy
* help more people, and a wider range of people, to take an active part in and make decisions about heritage.

It is open to all **not-for-profit** organizations, and there are no deadlines for applications under £5 million. Applications are assessed in two rounds and it takes 3 months or more for a decision. See the website: www.hlf.org.uk.

The looser grant application criteria are, the more organizations are likely to apply and the greater the competition is likely to be.

Ian Ferguson, Grants Advisor, Preston Council for Voluntary Services

The Big Lottery Fund

The Big Lottery Fund has the most money to give away

••

The Big Lottery Fund (www.biglotteryfund.org.uk) has the **biggest pot** and distributes close to half the money raised by the National Lottery. It also distributes money from other sources.

Grants from £300 to over £500,000 are available to small local groups as well as to major charities.

You can also apply for some of your **running costs** as well as the direct costs of your project, which many grant makers won't fund. These must relate to a specific project and can include salaries for project workers, **volunteers' expenses** and a dedicated laptop.

At the time of writing the Big Lottery Fund is running 31 programmes, which include Awards for All.

Other programmes include:

Name	Where	Grants
Village SOS	UK-wide	Supports business initiatives that bring people together in villages
Reaching Out: Connecting Older People	Northern Ireland only	Helps older people at risk to lead fuller, more connected lives as valued members of their community
Silver Dreams	England	A new, £10 million initiative, looking for projects that will pioneer ways of helping older people deal more effectively with life-changing events. A further £100 million will be rolled out through to 2015
Supporting 21st Century Life	Scotland	Projects that bring people together, create understanding and reduce isolation

Sport England

Sport England funds several programmes including:

* the Small Grants programme
* the Inspired Facilities programme.

The Small Grants programme gives grants between £300 and £10,000 for:

* new community projects
* growing or sustaining participation in sport
* supporting talent **development**.

It gives priority to projects that:

* increase the number of adults participating in sports
* reduce the drop-off rates for 16- to 19-year-olds in sports.

34

1 You will need to be a formally constituted not-for-profit organization to apply.
2 Your project should not cost more than £50,000.
3 Your project must also focus on sports recognized by Sport England.

Inspired Facilities focuses on:

* helping improve and refurbish **sports clubs**
* transforming non-sporting venues into sports facilities.

It is looking for projects that:

* offer **local opportunities** for people who don't currently play sport
* are the only public sports facility in the community.

Grants are worth between £20,000 and £50,000, and money will be available until 2014 when the last funding round takes place.

Applications can be made online. For further information see www.sportengland.org.

4 The big four

Other important sources of funding

Spread your net wide to increase your chances of gaining a grant

As well as the National Lottery there are other big **funding bodies**. Each has its own rules and requirements, but once you have assembled the material for one application you will find that you can adapt it for others.

Read through the **requirements** for each funder (you'll find the detail on their websites) and work out whether your project fits the bill.

In this chapter we will be looking at four major funders and what they give grants for:

* Comic Relief funds projects across a **broad range**.
* Children In Need focuses on children and young people.
* The Esmée Fairbairn Foundation concentrates on the arts, education, the environment and disadvantaged people.
* The Lloyds TSB Foundation funds projects for disadvantaged people.

Don't apply for **retrospective** funding as few bodies will consider it.

Comic Relief

In the UK Comic Relief funds grants directly (generally up to £40,000 a year), and also gives grants ranging from £1,000 to £10,000 through various programmes delivered by the Community Foundation Network on its behalf.

The charity raised more than £102 million in 2011, with all the money raised by the public, helping people with incredibly tough lives

It is particularly **keen** to fund projects that target areas and groups of people who often miss out, so will accept applications from the voluntary and community sector throughout the UK including:

* constituted voluntary and community groups
* charities
* social enterprises
* co-operatives
* faith organizations (the money cannot be used for religious purposes)
* community interest companies.

It will fund revenue costs such as **salaries** and capital costs such as office equipment.

You can also include some organizational **running costs** in your budget.

Areas it won't fund include:

- ☒ grants to individuals
- ☒ medical research or hospitals
- ☒ work where there is statutory responsibility to provide funding
- ☒ projects where the work has already taken place.

There are specific deadlines for applying for grants – see the website: www.comicrelief.com.

BBC Children in Need

BBC Children in Need is a national grant-giving organization that gives grants to organizations that work with **disadvantaged children** and young people under the age of 18 years in the UK. Such disadvantage includes:

* illness, distress, abuse or neglect
* any kind of disability
* behavioural or psychological difficulties
* living in poverty or situations of deprivation.

Under the general grants programme there are two funding streams:

1 small grants of £10,000 or less per year for up to 3 years
2 main grants of £10,000 or more per year for up to 3 years.

To qualify for any of the grants you need to be a registered charity or other **not-for-profit** organization.

In each grant round, organizations around the country are given grants to make children and young people's lives easier and happier.

CASE STUDY

The Let's Play Project in Banbury, Oxfordshire, was given £17,928 for a project that provides drama therapy for the siblings of disabled children. The children will use music, dance and drama to explore issues such as jealousy, loss, bereavement and conflict. They will also learn new skills and grow in confidence.

For full, up-to-date guidance on eligibility criteria and advice on how to apply, visit www.bbc.co.uk/pudsey/grants.

Esmée Fairbairn Foundation

This is one of the largest independent foundations in the country, and in 2010 it gave away £21.5 million in grants through the main fund – the average grant being **£79,774**.

It funds projects concerned with:

1 the arts
2 education
3 the environment
4 enabling disadvantaged people to participate fully in society.

It is keen to help projects that other grant makers may find **hard to fund**, such as those which:

* break new ground
* appear too risky
* require core funding

* need a more unusual form of financial help such as a loan.

It doesn't give grants for:

☒ capital costs
☒ health care

☒ animal welfare
☒ retrospective funding.

It will consider requests to fund core or project costs, including running costs such as staff salaries and overheads

↓

You do not have to be a registered charity to apply, but the project must be legally charitable and your constitution must also allow you to carry out the work you propose

↓

There is a two-stage application process, which can be done online. The first stage asks for an outline proposal and you will hear within a month whether you can make a second-stage application or you have been declined

There is plenty of helpful information on the website: www.esmeefairbairn.org.uk.

Lloyds TSB Foundation

The Lloyds TSB Foundation (www.lloydstsbfoundation.com) is one of the UK's leading independent grant-making trusts, and gives grants to **registered charities** that help disadvantaged people play a fuller role in the community through:

* improved social and community involvement
* improved life choices and chances
* helping them to be heard.

What it won't fund includes:

- ☒ capital projects
- ☒ environmental work
- ☒ health research
- ☒ work with animals.

Applications can be made at any time, and you can expect a decision after 3–6 months, depending on the size of the grant.

The application process is slightly different from that of other funders. Charities are asked to complete an online eligibility form to find out if their request may be eligible for funding.

Once this is completed, charities are advised whether they have been successful and, if they are, a grant manager will visit the charity to discuss the request in further detail and then advise whether or not to apply for funding.

If successful, you will have to submit a **grant report** for each year of your grant with a breakdown of how you have spent the money against your planned budget.

There are separate foundations in Scotland, the Channel Islands and Northern Ireland.

5 Local grants

Looking locally

Local grants are often overlooked, but they can provide additional or matching funding

Some nationwide funders now have **geographical priorities** and will give money only to deprived areas – other funders will give only to local or regional projects.

It's always worth checking if local authorities have, or know of, general grants to support community activities in your area, regardless of the specific activity you have in mind, e.g. sport, arts, heritage, health, etc.

Ian Ferguson, Grants Advisor, Preston Council for Voluntary Services

In this chapter we will look at the different types of **local funding** and how to find it. As well as handling affairs for large charities such as Comic Relief, Community Foundation Network members also have wide knowledge of what is available locally.

The Landfill Communities Fund is specifically for projects within a certain distance of landfill sites, which can be found in many parts of the country. Similarly, the Coal Regeneration Trust gives grants for projects in eligible coalfield areas.

Other funders, such as Wessex Water and Heathrow Airport, will give grants only in their **geographical area**.

This chapter also covers methods of finding local funders via the Internet.

The Community Foundation Network

The Community Foundation Network (www.communityfoundations.org) is a registered charity and also the national membership association for 56 community foundations covering most of the UK. It **administers funds** on behalf of other funders and gives grants to small voluntary and community groups for:

1 arts and culture
2 education
3 environment
4 health
5 community development
6 children and young people
7 older people
8 employment and training.

Each community foundation sets its own *priorities* and reviews them frequently. Not all foundations fund all of the areas above.

Some community foundations have many funds from which to make grants. Either they will advise you on the most appropriate fund to apply to or they may have a common application form for all of their funds.

What they are unlikely to fund are:

* work outside the local area
* major capital appeals
* **standard** appeal letters
* projects and services with an exclusively religious purpose
* party political applications.

Details of local foundations can be found on the website. Each one has **an advisor** to help applicants.

Finding local funders

You can use the Internet by putting the key words 'charitable trusts' or 'charitable foundations' followed by the name of your county into a search engine. The websites that this method throws up could well be **small funders** who give only small local grants – but 10 small grants could add up to a significant part of your budget.

Individual Masonic Lodges also make donations to **local charities**, and your local Round Table and Lions groups may be able to help.

Or you can use the Charity Commission's register to find local funders.

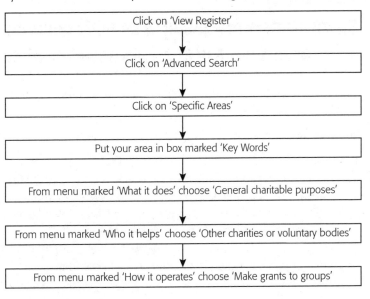

Click on 'View Register'

Click on 'Advanced Search'

Click on 'Specific Areas'

Put your area in box marked 'Key Words'

From menu marked 'What it does' choose 'General charitable purposes'

From menu marked 'Who it helps' choose 'Other charities or voluntary bodies'

From menu marked 'How it operates' choose 'Make grants to groups'

Regional funders
Some funders are based in specific geographical area, others give grants based on eligibility

You can use the Internet search method to find **regional funders** by replacing county names with regional ones.

Regional funders include:

1 Wessex Watermarks Scheme (www.wessexwater.co.uk), managed by the Conservation Foundation, gives grants up to £1,500 for **environmental projects** within the Wessex Water region.
2 The Ballinger Charitable Trust (www.ballingercharitabletrust.org.uk) gives grants for projects in the north-east of England.
3 The Coalfields Regeneration Trust (www.coalfields-regen.org.uk) gives grants for projects based in **eligible** coalfield communities.
4 Major airports – several give grants to projects within their vicinity.

There are also databases for finding regional funding:

TOP TIP
When looking on company websites you may have to put 'grants' in the search box because information about them is not always shown on the main pages.

* www.fine.org.uk, which gives **funding information** including a database of trusts and foundations that give grants in the north-east of England as well as nationwide

* www.syfab.or.uk, South Yorkshire Funding Advice Bureau, which is designed for voluntary and **community organizations** in South Yorkshire, but also includes major charitable trusts

* www.cvsfife.org, which has a **database** of funders in the Fife area as well as nationally.

Be innovative and keep researching. There are still different funders out there who have money to give and which haven't yet been approached.

Ray Emmans, Fund Manager, Windsor and Maidenhead Voluntary Action

Landfill Communities Fund

This is a government scheme to provide funding for community and environmental projects in the vicinity of **landfill sites**.

Companies that run the landfill sites are taxed on the amount of waste they dispose of. They can give a proportion of this tax to the Landfill Communities Fund and receive a tax credit in return.

ENTRUST regulates the fund on behalf of HM Revenue and Customs. It does not fund any work itself.

Projects must achieve specific objectives including:

- ☑ restoration of land
- ☑ reduction in pollution
- ☑ provision or improvement of a **public amenity**
- ☑ **protection** of a species or its environment
- ☑ restoration of religious or historic buildings.

There are two ways of claiming grants:

1 registering with ENTRUST as an environmental body (EB)
2 applying to a distributive environmental body (DEB).

The **criteria** for registering as an EB can be found on the ENTRUST website (www.entrust.org.uk). A list of DEBs can be found on the site under **Finding Funding**.

Some DEBs fund in one geographical area and some will fund across the country. They all have different priorities, and some require you to **enrol** with ENTRUST before receiving a grant.

The Association of Distributive and Environmental Bodies (www.adebmembers.org.uk) is the representative body of EBs and DEBs and its website also lists details of its members.

6 Popular projects

Focus your grant application

Some types of project, or parts of them, are more popular than others

In this section we will look at the funders who give money for some of the most **popular ones**, principally the arts, sports, the environment, community, and projects run by young people.

Break your budget down into different parts and apply to different funders for each one.

Arsen Poghosyan, Funding and Information Officer,
Brentwood Council for Voluntary Services

The Arts Council is the biggest funder of **arts projects**. Sports funding is spread across a number of bodies, as is funding for environmental projects. Heritage and community projects are mostly funded by National Lottery money. **Young people** who want to make a difference should look at the Prince's Trust and O2.

Your project may fit into more than one category, so be prepared to make **several applications**. Some funding bodies cover many types of project; some, such as the Football Foundation, have a narrow focus, others, such as the Naturesave Trust, have a broader remit.

If you aren't sure whether your project qualifies, make contact with the organization and ask for advice.

Arts and sport

County adult community services may fund art and sporting projects that help people of all ages to take part – check your local authority's website.

Lottery funding is also available for the arts from the Arts Council:

Arts-related activities funded	Who is eligible?	Grants
Projects and events Commissions and productions Research and development Activities for people to take part in Audience development Professional development Touring	Individuals, such as artists, performers and writers Arts organizations Unincorporated groups and charities	Range from £1,000 to £100,000, but at least 10% of the project's cost must come from other sources

Applications can be submitted online: see the Arts Council website (www.artscouncil.org.uk), which also has information on other arts funders.

The National Lottery is not the only avenue to explore for sports funding.

The Football Foundation (www.footballfoundation.co.uk) is the UK's largest sports charity and funds several initiatives including:

* **GrassRoots** – facilities for community benefit
* Build the Game – for pitch and stadia improvement.

Cash 4 Clubs (www.cash-4-clubs.com) offers all **community sports clubs** in the UK the chance to win grants ranging from £250 to £1,000 for improving facilities and buying equipment.

The environment

The first port of call for environmental grants should be **county councils** – they have been tasked by the government to fund green issues so should have money for environmental projects.

You can also try:

* The Environmental Funders Network (www.greenfunders.org), which lists on its website more than 60 trusts and foundations that give grants for environmental and **conservation issues**.
* The Energy Efficient Venues, which is a Big Lottery Fund programme (www.biglotteryfund.org.uk) that gives grants to community organizations to carry out work at their venues to make them more **environmentally friendly** and energy efficient.

Do your research before you apply for grants.

Martha Langley, volunteer with various mental health charities

The Naturesave Trust (www.naturesave.co.uk) funds projects that specifically address:

1 sustainable development
2 **environmental**, conservation and green issues.

It funds charities, voluntary organizations and businesses and prefers to provide **start-up capital** for small projects rather than general administration costs. There are no deadlines for applications and no limit on the number you can make.

The Heritage Lottery Fund (www.hlf.org.uk) has programmes for improving the environment including:

1 Parks for People, which funds projects that regenerate public parks of national, regional or **local heritage** value
2 Landscape Partnership, which funds projects to conserve or restore built and natural features that create the **historic landscape** character.

Community
Some funders include community projects in their remit, others give grants specifically for them

Reaching Communities is a Big Lottery Fund programme for England only, which funds projects that help people and **communities in most need**. It is of particular interest to voluntary and community organizations, and will fund revenue and small- and large-capital projects, with grants between £10,000 and £500,000, for projects that address four issues:

1 giving people a better chance in life to improve their **life skills**
2 creating stronger communities
3 improving the rural and urban environments
4 creating healthier and more active people and communities.

The Big Local Trust programme is investing up to £200 million over the next 10 years in up to 150 urban and rural neighbourhoods, across England only, which have been overlooked for funding in the past.

Bullet Guide: Successful Grant Applications

The Foyle Foundation (www.foylefoundation.org.uk) has a Small Grants Scheme offering grants from £1,000 to £10,000 to support **smaller charities** in the UK working at grass roots and local community level.

Projects can cover a wide range of activities, but applicants must show that a grant would make a significant difference to their success.

Applications can be made at any time, but it can take up to 4 months to obtain a decision.

Young people's projects

The Prince's Trust (www.princes-trust.org.uk) gives Community Cash Awards of up to £3,000 to design and set up new **youth-led** projects in England and Wales.

Many young people feel strongly about their community and want to do something to improve it

Your project must:

- ☑ benefit the local community
- ☑ benefit the people running the project
- ☑ help you to develop new skills for your future.

The Heritage Lottery Fund's **Young Roots** programme provides 13- to 25-year-olds with opportunities to learn about their own and others' heritage. It allows them to **lead and take part** in creative activities and provides opportunities for gaining skills in identifying, interpreting and caring for heritage. For further information and application details go to www.hlf.org.uk.

O2 (www.o2thinkbig.co.uk) wants young people to think big and then bigger. It gives grants to those aged 13–25 in the UK who want to improve their community.

Submit an idea and the O2 team will help you develop it

↓

Apply for an initial grant of £300 and you will get training or support to get you started

↓

If that goes well you might be able to apply for a further grant of up to £2,500

↓

The website is easy to use and you can **upload photos and videos** to show off your achievements

↓

You should hear in 6 weeks if you have been successful and your project could be up and running within a couple of months

7 Finding further funding

Looking for more grants

There is plenty of advice and information available to help you find further funding

....

Although it is easy to find websites for the best known and most popular funders, the others are more difficult to track down. There are **no short cuts** to finding grants – it is a case of leaving no stone unturned.

But there is help out there. Some databases, such as the **Directory of Grant Making Trusts**, are available in reference libraries, others can be found online. There are also organizations that can give help and advice.

In this chapter we will look at the services offered by The National Association for Voluntary and Community Action (NAVCA), which has branches all over England and Wales. Scotland and Northern Ireland have their own organizations.

We will also look at the **databases** available online – some free, some partly paid for and some by subscription only. The fees are from £25 (plus VAT) upwards depending on the services offered and the range of grant makers listed.

Some NAVCA groups pay the subscription for some databases that you can then access for free.

Use the resources at your local library to track down local organizations.

Martha Langley, volunteer with various mental health charities

National Association for Voluntary and Community Action

NAVCA (www.navca.org.uk) is a country-wide association of more than 400 local support and development organizations, which help local charities, voluntary organizations and community groups.

Because of their **expertise and knowledge** they can help with:

1 finding funding
2 setting up committees
3 filling in grant application forms
4 organizing training.

They also provide practical information, advice and guidance on public service delivery, and because of their local knowledge they can:

- ☑ spread good practice
- ☑ prevent duplication of effort
- ☑ help groups make **effective use** of resources
- ☑ encourage more people to volunteer
- ☑ provide a forum for voluntary and community groups.

To find your local group click on 'Members Directory' for local contacts. Their websites will show what help and **facilities** they can offer because not all NAVCA members offer the same things. Go to www.scvo.org.uk for groups in Scotland and www.nicva.org for groups in Northern Ireland.

Some are run by part-time staff so it may take a couple of phone calls to get through. If your nearest NAVCA member is unable to help, he or she should be able to tell you who can.

Free databases
Start by using the free databases – if you can't find funders there, then turn to the paid ones
. . . .

* The National Council for Voluntary Organisations (www.ncvo-vol.org. uk) gives support and advice on how to apply for grants and also produces the directory Funding Central (www.fundingcentral.org.uk). This is a **free database** for charities, voluntary organizations and social enterprises and is easy to use, giving access to thousands of funding and finance opportunities, plus tools and resources.

* GRANTnet (www.grantnet.com) has a database of more than 4,000 funding opportunities for charitable and community groups and allows access to **information** on what is available locally as well as nationally and in Europe. Putting in your postcode and clicking on 'community' links you with a local 'host organization' that will give further assistance.

78

The Association of Charitable Foundations (www.acf.org.uk) has a membership of around 300 large and small funders, which are listed on its website:

1 Click on 'Trusts and foundations' in the side menu.
2 Click on 'Find out about ACF member trusts and foundations'.
3 Click on 'Links to ACF member trusts and foundations'.

TOP TIP
Not all websites are updated so some funders may no longer exist and others may have changed their details.

Databases costing less than £100

J4B Community (www.j4bcommunity.co.uk) Registration is free and allows a search for funding but with **limited access** to information. You will have to pay £49.99 to see further details. The website is easy to use and searching is by **sector and location**. It also gives information on current available funding and deadlines for applying, as well as email grant alerts when new funds are launched and reminders about approaching deadlines.

Access Funds (www.accessfunds.co.uk) Has a database of grant makers including government, charitable trusts and European Union funders. A 12 month subscription costs £50, which also includes a monthly round-up of **latest grant programmes** and an email alert service giving details of the latest funding information.

Funding Information (www.fundinginformation.org) Gives information on the **latest grants** from charitable trusts and foundations, central government, the National Lottery, Europe, and companies. Its 'grant of the week' highlights a **new source** of funding. It offers a reduced annual subscription rate (for organizations with an annual income of less than £50,000) of £100 plus VAT or a 1 month subscription for £40.

Grants Online (www.grantsonline.org.uk) Gives information on grants from the European Union, the National Lottery, the government and grant-making trusts and foundations. Information is updated daily and 1 month's subscription is £25.

Although not an online database, the Directory of Grant Making Trusts is available to buy online, current price £125.

Databases costing more than £100

Directory of Social Change (www.dsc.org.uk) An independent charity that provides information and training for the voluntary sector to help groups find funding. It also publishes subscription databases on its website.

Name	Website	Details on database	Cost
Trust Funding	www.trustfunding.org.uk	4,500 trusts and foundations	£250
Company Giving	www.companygiving.org.uk	Gives information on companies and on making an approach for corporate partnership	£250
Government Funding	www.governmentfunding.org.uk	Offers regional, local and national government funding opportunities. Also keeps you updated on funding rounds coming up	£225

82

GRANTfinder (www.grantfinder.co.uk) More than 6,000 **funding opportunities**. The information is easy to access and constantly updated. It also lists forthcoming deadlines for applications for funds that may be undersubscribed. The subscription cost depends on the level of your requirement.

CASE STUDY

When applying for a grant, get as many people as you can to **write letters** explaining the importance of the project. Attach these letters to the application so that the grant maker can see what it means to the community.

We did this in our village and they not only said what a difference it made, but also came to the opening of our hall.

Sheila Davidson

8 Writing a grant application

The nuts and bolts of an application

Making a grant application can seem daunting, but if you're organized and methodical you will get through it

There are **no short cuts** to writing a grant application, so set time aside for the task, and don't try to do it all in one session. Start by gathering up all the documents you need, then work through the form step by step. If you're applying by letter, expect to write several drafts. Remember to keep copies of everything you send out – you don't want to approach the same funder twice.

Create a timetable so that you meet the deadline. Read the **requirements** before you start, and double-check them before you send your application. Answer all the questions, and check with your contact at the funder if you aren't sure about anything.

Show the funder that your group is both enthusiastic and **efficient** – no one will give you money if you are well meaning but woolly. If they make you a grant, remember to say thank you and to stay in touch.

TOP TIP
Try to establish a one-to-one relationship with someone at the grant-making body.

Be prepared

There are no short cuts to writing a grant application. You have to get it right because you may only get one bite of the cherry

Grant application forms vary from funder to funder. Some are long and complicated, others are **user-friendly**. Some funders have a two-stage system, others require just a simple letter. But each funder will expect its **requirements** to be met.

Some of the requirements may seem **onerous**, but it is their money and if they want you to jump through hoops, then that is what you must do.

TOP TIP
Remember, there are more applicants looking for money than there is money to be given away.

Although application forms will vary, there are common elements, so have these prepared in advance including:

1. the **minutes** of your first meeting
2. your constitution
3. your business plan
4. your budget
5. a set of **accounts**
6. bank statements.

If you keep all these documents together and up to date, then it is easy for someone else to step in and take over the application process if necessary.

Sally Dubery, chief officer, Voluntary Action Mid Surrey

TOP TIP

Take several photocopies of the main documents so that, if one funder turns you down, you are ready to send off another application immediately.

Getting it right

If you followed the advice in Chapter 2, you should have a list of possible funders. The next stage is to check the following:

1. their **guidelines** – most fund makers have them available online
2. their criteria – does your project meets their **requirements**?
3. their **deadlines** – do they have a rolling programme or specific dates?
4. do they accept applications online or by post?
5. what documents they need – and what they don't need
6. how long you have to wait for a reply.

> **TOP TIP**
> Check who will be dealing with your application and get to know them if you can – some funders are keen to do this, others may not be.

It is also time to get your budget right.

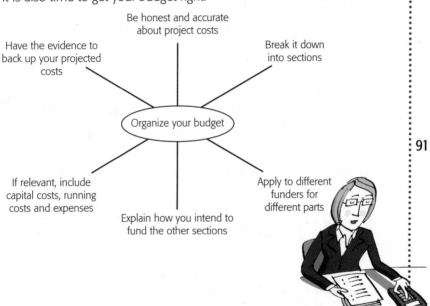

Be honest and accurate
about project costs

Have the evidence to
back up your projected
costs

Break it down
into sections

Organize your budget

If relevant, include
capital costs, running
costs and expenses

Explain how you intend to
fund the other sections

Apply to different
funders for
different parts

The application

Answer all the questions. If you don't understand one, contact the funder and ask – don't guess!

Don't

✗ Include **unnecessary** information.
✗ Include jargon or specialist words.
✗ Miss the deadline.

Do

✔ Show that you will be delivering **value for money**.
✔ Double-check and ask others to check your answers.
✔ Keep a copy of your application and any other documents you send.
✔ Include the name of your group, **a contact name**, address and phone number.

TOP TIP
Make copies of the form – if you make a mistake, you still have blank ones to fill in correctly.

Some funders may want only a letter to start with, or you may be asked to explain your project as part of the application.

Make a list of everything you want to include in it:

* In the opening paragraphs explain who you are and what your group wants to **achieve** – don't assume that the funder will know this.
* Highlight what makes it **distinctive**, how many people it will **benefit** – and, most importantly, what will happen if the project doesn't go ahead.
* The closing paragraph should be a **summary** of your appeal.

TOP TIP
Be enthusiastic – if you aren't keen on your project, you can't expect a funder to be.

The decision

* Waiting for a decision is tedious, but it can't be hurried. Many funders don't have full-time staff. Some trustees meet only once or twice a year to look at applications.
* Don't keep ringing to find out if you have been successful. Spend the time looking for other funders in case you haven't been.
* When the good news comes, **say thank you**.

Once you have your money, your responsibilities to the funder haven't ended. If they want to keep in contact, then take the time to keep them updated.

Check with them. Would they like:

* regular reports and photos?
* **media** coverage?
* an invitation to the opening?
* a **plaque** put up?

Funders would rather know if things are going wrong so let them know if:

1 you run into **problems**
2 you make any changes to the project, even small ones
3 you have to delay the **completion date**.

Finally, when your project is up and running let them know how well it is doing and how much their money is **appreciated**.

9 Handling rejection

The funder says no

Rejection is unpleasant, but don't take it personally – it isn't you that's being rejected

No one likes being rejected, but when it comes to applying for grants it is bound to happen at some point.

Sometimes it is not your **fault** – a funder has already had too many applicants, or may have already funded a **similar project** in your area. Sometimes it's down to an error or **misunderstanding** on your part. The **secret** is not to let it stop you achieving your goal.

So take a deep breath and move on, because in this chapter we will be looking at ways of **overcoming** rejection. Try to find out why your project was rejected – was it because you didn't read the **guidelines** properly, or because you applied to the wrong funder?

Redrafting your application to show new funders a different aspect of your project is one option, or breaking it into sections and applying for several grants is another.

Re-energize

Knowledge is power, so find out what went wrong. The more information you have, the more likely you can remedy the problem.

1 **Read** the rejection letter thoroughly – it may tell you why you were turned down.
2 **Contact** the person you have been dealing with and ask them for more details. This is where creating a relationship can help.
3 **Don't ignore** any useful feedback or a request for more information. If you are asked to jump through another hoop, do it.
4 **Thank** them for letting you know why it failed and ask if you could reapply in the future – their criteria may change down the line.

> **TOP TIP**
> Use rejection positively, not negatively.

Sometimes rejection is not your fault. The funder may have:

* had **too many** applicants for their money
* already funded a similar project in your area
* **changed** their criteria.

But whatever the reason, it's straight back to the drawing board:

1 If you have a list of other possible funders, **get straight on** to the next application.
2 If you don't, start researching again – a new source of funding may have become available.
3 Look again at funders you originally crossed off your list – they may have changed their criteria.
4 **Re-read** their guidelines – perhaps you misunderstood what they will and won't fund?

Recheck

Look objectively at your application – despite all your research did you approach the wrong funder or did you ask them to fund aspects which were outside their criteria?

CASE STUDY

My first approach to Awards for All was an application for a £10,000 grant to cover operating expenses. However, that application was unsuccessful as it doesn't award funds for expenses. Later I reapplied, this time for a specific project that satisfied their criteria, and Awards for All granted us the full amount.

Matthew Robinson, fundraiser for a national support helpline

Error	Solution
Applied for retrospective funding – funders usually won't give grants for work already carried out and paid for	**Increase** fundraising activities to cover cash shortfalls
Applied for costs that were formerly paid by local or central government	**Look for other funders** who are prepared to cover these costs
Project not sustainable	**Revise** your projected budget and put plans in place for future funding
Missed the deadline	Reapply in next funding round or find another funder

Redraft

People have to be open minded about their project and be prepared to look at other alternatives for funding.

Sally Dubery, chief officer, Voluntary Action Mid Surrey

Funders' guidelines may be more **elastic** than you realize so perhaps it is time to **think outside the box**.

Look again at your project and try to **tweak** it to show new funders a different aspect that fits their criteria.

You may have been concentrating on the main aim of your project – to build a village hall, for example – but have been turned down for a full grant, so make a list of what **benefits** will come from your proposal.

In this case the list will include:

1 An **energy-efficient** building will improve the environment.
2 A dedicated recording studio will get **young people** off the street.
3 A sports hall will encourage people to take up **exercise**.
4 A kitchen will give the **elderly** and lonely a lunch once a week.
5 A social room will give **mums and babies** somewhere to meet.

This project could now attract grants from five completely different funding bodies.

The same exercise can be applied to most projects – it's just a question of looking at it through **different eyes**.

> **TOP TIP**
> Don't change the project to fit the funder – find another funder.

Reassess

You may find yourself in the situation in which funders won't commit unless you already have other grants in place

Grants from other funders demonstrates to trusts and foundations that other granting bodies have **faith** in your project, which, in turn, gives them confidence to hand over their money. The difficulty is in getting that **first offer**.

At one time local authorities were able to give grants to get the **ball rolling**, but cutbacks have ended that in most areas. However, offers in kind such as a rent-free room or photocopying facilities may be enough to persuade a funder that a constituted body has checked out your project and is satisfied with it.

Other ideas to try:

- ☑ Apply for several smaller grants rather than one large one – small grants are easier to get.
- ☑ Do **more fundraising** to show your commitment to your project (see Chapter 10) – funders want to see that you are making every effort.
- ☑ **Get help** with writing your application. For large grants it may pay to use professionals.

Success breeds success, and having even one grant offer could tip the balance in your favour.

Tony Moulin, chairman of YACWAG

If you are consistently getting rejected, then consider whether your project is **really needed** – or whether the need is being met by other groups.

10 Matching funding

Funding from other sources

Not all projects can be financed entirely from grants

Unless you are lucky enough to get one or more grants to cover the cost of your project, you will have to find money from **other sources**.

Some funders specify that there has to be matching funding in place before they will give a grant. This shows them that your project has the **support** of other funders, businesses and benefactors and is therefore safe to invest in.

There are several ways of finding money from other sources. In this chapter we will be looking at:

* fundraising – both tried and trusted methods as well as **new technology**
* non-cash contributions – turning volunteers' hours and offers of help into a **cash equivalent**
* raising loans from your supporters and the community to be paid back later
* taking out **business loans** from banks
* the importance of targeting sponsors
* what donors want in return for their money.

Fundraising

When it comes to raising money there is room for both traditional methods and new technology

People will usually give money if you are offering them something they would have paid for anyway, so use your talents to make, or produce, items for sale.

Don't despise tried and trusted fundraising ideas – they are usually cheap and simple to do, and they make money.

Talent	Make money by
Cooking	Selling home-made cakes, jams and chutneys
Green fingers	Selling surplus plants, fruit and vegetables
Hospitality	Holding coffee mornings, tea afternoons and gourmet dinners
Sewing	Making alterations to clothes

You can also use new technology to help raise money:

* Advertise your events on Facebook or Twitter.
* Set up a PayPal account (www.paypal.co.uk).
* Set up an online page with Just Giving (www.justgiving.com).

CASE STUDY

I wanted to do a sponsored walk for our local multiple sclerosis centre. I mentioned it on Facebook and lots of people contacted me wanting to send a donation. I then set up an online page with Just Giving, and to let people know I put a link on Facebook. It started slowly and then grew with donations coming in from all over the world. It was absolutely brilliant.

Sarah Boyce

Non-cash contributions

* Many businesses find it pays to be seen doing something for the community – whether locally or nationally – and they encourage their staff to do **voluntary work**. So tap into this resource.
* The number of hours they give helping with your project can be shown as cash, and some funders will accept this as **matching funding**. Even if each hour they do is counted as worth the minimum wage, it all adds up.
* Check the websites of national banks, supermarkets or nationwide businesses for their schemes. If they have a branch in your area, you have a better chance of success.

Contributions in kind also count. It is easy to work out what the following would cost if you had to pay, and this can be added to your matching funding:

1 any **printing**, such as for leaflets
2 use of facilities such as office space
3 advertising space in the media.

Make a list of items needed for your project, and ask local people and businesses to buy them for you.

Loans

If your project is capable of generating income when it is completed, it might be worthwhile considering taking out a loan to make up a shortfall in money. This could be a commercial one via a bank or a **local initiative** relying on supporters.

> ### CASE STUDY
>
> As our proposed village hall would be able to generate an income, we asked local people to give interest-free loans of £100 each to be paid back within 2 years. It was so successful that we raised more money than we needed.
>
> Ann Gawthorpe, former treasurer, Claverham Village Hall Building Committee

Local businesses might also give **interest-free loans** in return for publicity.

If you go down the commercial route, you must have a good business plan and be able to show what your project's future income will be and how you will pay back the loan. If your project owns property, you might be able to use that as **collateral**.

If you are a registered charity and raising a mortgage, you should check the Charity Commission's website for special requirements.

There are **specialist banks** that deal with charities and make loans such as the Charities Aid Foundation (www.cafonline.org), which offers banking facilities for charities and loans or capital. The Esmée Fairbairn Foundation (www.esmeefairbairn.org.uk) will also fund loans.

Donations and sponsorship

Because companies can claim tax relief on money they donate to charities, some will already have a certain sum set aside for **donations**.

If you intend on approaching local businesses that are new to this, they may need to check on the HM Revenue and Customs website (www. hmrc.gov.uk) for advice on what tax they can claim back.

It is also common for businesses to sponsor charities and voluntary groups, but the **tax relief** they can claim from this is different from giving a donation and depends on the nature of the sponsorship. Again, check the HM Revenue and Customs website.

- ☑ It pays to **target** your potential sponsors – you are more likely to get sponsorship for an animal rescue centre from a company selling pet food than from one selling paint.
- ☑ Sponsors will also be looking for **free publicity** in return for their money, particularly in the media. So be prepared to spend time on sending out press releases thanking them for their help.
- ☑ They may also want some form of **acknowledgement** in the finished project, such as a board with their name or logo on it.
- ☑ Always be generous with your **thanks** because you may want to go back to funders for more money.

Good luck!

Further reading

Applying to a Grant Making Trust by Anne Villemur (Charities Aid Foundation, 1996).

Fundraising for a Community Project by Simon Whaley (How to Books Ltd, 2007).

Books are also available from:

National Council for Voluntary Organisations (www.ncvo-vol.org.uk)

Directory of Social Change (www.dsc.org.uk)